SPICE GIRLS

Exclusive Distributors:
Music Sales Limited, 8/9 Frith Street, London W1V 5TZ, England.
Music Sales Pty Limited, 120 Rothschild Avenue, Rosebery, NSW 2018, Australia.

Order No.AM940951
ISBN 0-7119-6149-2
This book © Copyright 1996 by Wise Publications
Visit the Internet Music Shop at http://www.musicsales.co.uk

Music arranged by Jason Hazeley.
Music processed by Paul Ewers Music Design.
Photographs courtesy of Francessca Sorrenti.
Printed in the United Kingdom by
Printwise (Haverhill) Limited, Haverhill, Suffolk.

Your Guarantee of Quality:
As publishers, we strive to produce every book to the highest commercial standards.
The music has been freshly engraved and, whilst endeavouring to retain the original running order of the recorded album,
the book has been carefully designed to minimise awkward page turns and to make playing from it a real pleasure.
Particular care has been given to specifying acid-free, neutral-sized paper made from pulps which have not been elemental chlorine bleached.
This pulp is from farmed sustainable forests and was produced with special regard for the environment.
Throughout, the printing and binding have been planned to ensure a sturdy, attractive publication which should give years of enjoyment.
If your copy fails to meet our high standards, please inform us and we will gladly replace it.

Music Sales' complete catalogue describes thousands of titles and
is available in full colour sections by subject, direct from Music Sales Limited.
Please state your areas of interest and send a cheque/postal order for £1.50 for postage to:
Music Sales Limited, Newmarket Road, Bury St. Edmunds, Suffolk IP33 3YB.

Wise Publications
London / New York / Sydney / Paris / Copenhagen / Madrid

wannabe

**Words & Music by Matthew Rowbottom, Richard Stannard,
Melanie Brown, Victoria Aadams, Geri Halliwell, Emma Bunton & Melanie Chisholm.**

tell you what I want, what I real-ly real-ly want, so

tell me what you want, what you real-ly real-ly want. I wan-na,

I wan-na, I wan-na, I wan-na, I wan-na real-ly real-ly real-ly wan-na zig-a-zig ha.

If you wan-na be my lov-er, you got-ta get with my friends.

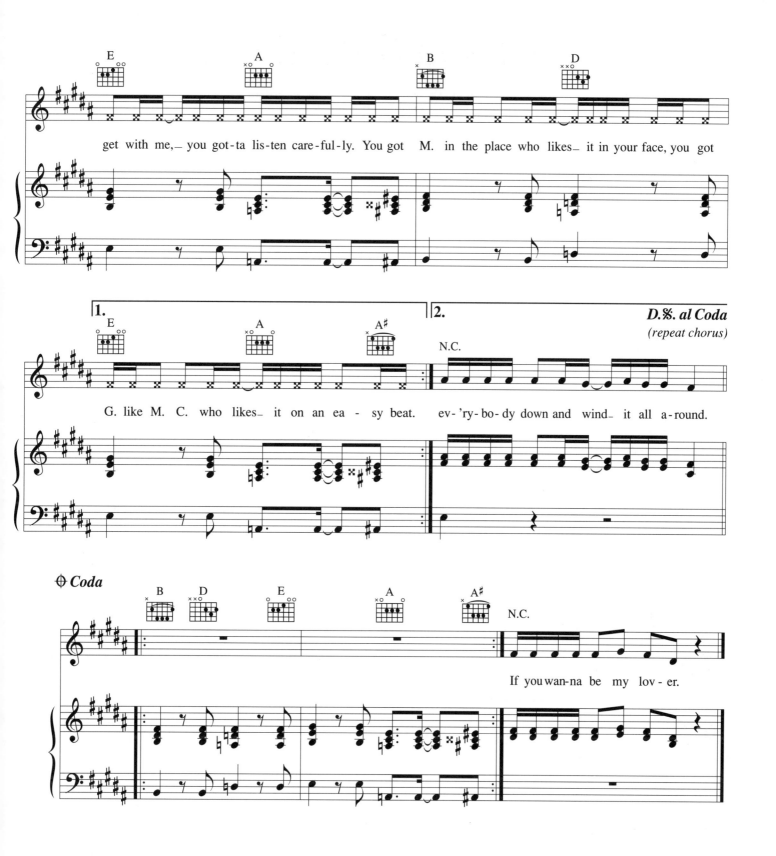

Verse 2:
What do you think about that now you know how I feel
Say you can handle my love, are you for real?
I won't be hasty, I'll give you a try
If you really bug me then I'll say goodbye.

say you'll be there

Words & Music by Eliot Kennedy, Melanie Brown, Victoria Aadams,
Geri Halliwell, Emma Bunton & Melanie Chisholm.

that we had— this con-ver-sa-tion I de-ci-ded we should be friends,_____ yeah.

But now we're go-ing round— in cir-cles tell me will this dé-jà vu nev-er end.—

Oh now you tell me that you've fall-en in love— well I nev-
(Verses 2 & 3 see block lyric)

-er ev-er thought that would be,_____ yeah. This time you

Verse 2:

If you put two and two together you will see what our friendship is for,
If you can't work this equation then I guess I'll have to show you the door,
There is no need to say you love me it would be better left unsaid.

I'm giving you everything all that joy can bring this I swear,
And all that I want from you is a promise you will be there,
Yeah I want you.

Verse 3: (Instrumental)
Any fool can see they're falling, gotta make you understand.
To Coda

2 become 1

Words & Music by Matthew Rowbottom, Richard Stannard,
Melanie Brown, Victoria Aadams, Geri Halliwell, Emma Bunton & Melanie Chisholm.

1. Can-dle light_ and soul_ for-ev-er a dream of you and me__ to-ge-ther.
(Verse 2 see block lyric)

Say you be-lieve_ it, say you be-lieve_ it. Free your mind_ of doubt_ and dan-ger,

had a lit-tle love now I'm back for more, (wan-na make love to ya ba-by.)

Set your spi-rit free,— it's the on-ly way— to be.————

Oh,———————— oh,——————

Verse 2:

Silly games that you were playing, empty words we both were saying,
Let's work it out boy, let's work it out boy.
Any deal that we endeavour, boys and girls feel good together,
Take it or leave it, take it or leave it.
Are you as good as I remember baby, get it on, get it on,
'Cause tonight is the night when two become one.

I need some love like I never needed love before, (wanna make love to ya baby.)
I had a little love, now I'm back for more, (wanna make love to ya baby.)
Set your spirit free, it's the only way to be.

love thing

Words & Music by Eliot Kennedy, Melanie Brown, Victoria Aadams,
Geri Halliwell, Emma Bunton, Melanie Chisholm & Cary Baylis.

don't wan - na know____ a - bout that love thing.

1. Been bro - ken heart - ed be - fore,____ oh, but that's the last____ time it
(Verses 2 & 3 see block lyric)

hap - pens to me,____ yeah,____ I keep on giv - ing, still you're ask - ing for more.

Too much e - mo - tion ba - by, why can't____ you see, I'm not a - fraid of your love,____

Verse 2:
Now don't go wasting my time, you're not the only thing I've got on my mind,
My friends are with me when you ain't been around,
Your precious words and promises ain't bringin' me down,
I've got some living to do, don't assume I'm gonna be with you,
You gotta want boy,
You know you got boy,
You gotta want me,
It's just what I need,
I'm not that easy as a matter of fact.

There's no room for lovin' stop that push and shovin' yeah...

Verse 3:(Spoken)
Stop pushing, you're rushing, you're losing my lovin'.
I hope it, I see it, just play it, you feel it.
Gotta be bold, bold and oh so strong,
Get with this and you got it goin' on,
On and on with the girls named Spice,
You wanna get with us then you'd better think twice,
God help the mister, yeah god help the mister,
That comes between me and my sisters,

(Sung)
I'm not afraid of your love,
I'm not afraid of your love, why can't you see I've had my share of that,
You're what I want boy,
You know you got boy,
You gotta want me,
It's just what I need,
I'm not that easy as a matter of fact,

There's no room for lovin', stop that push and shovin' yeah...

mama

Words & Music by Matthew Rowbottom, Richard Stannard,
Melanie Brown, Victoria Aadams, Geri Halliwell, Emma Bunton & Melanie Chisholm.

2. I

But now— I'm sure I know why,— why you were mis-un-der-stood.—

So now— I see through your eyes,—

all I can give—— you is love.——

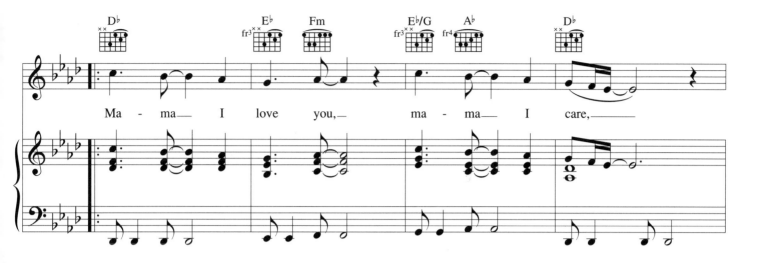

Ma - ma I love you, ma - ma I care,

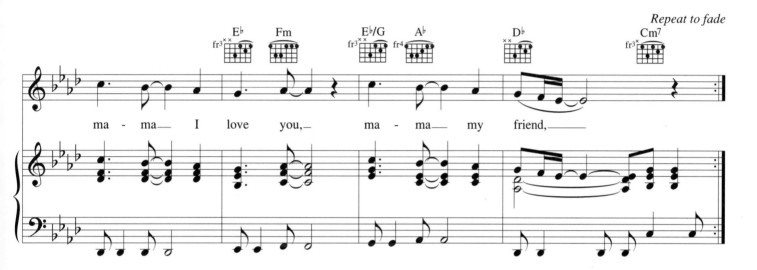

Repeat to fade

ma - ma I love you, ma - ma my friend,

Verse 2:

I didn't want to hear it then but I'm not ashamed to say it now,
Every little thing you said and did was right for me.
I had a lot of time to think about, about the way I used to be,
Never had a sense of my responsibility.

Back then I didn't know why, why you were misunderstood.
So now I see through your eyes, all that you did was love.
Mama I love you, Mama I care,
Mama I love you, Mama my friend,
My friend.

last time lover

Words & Music by Paul Wilson, Andy Watkins, Melanie Brown,
Victoria Aadams, Geri Halliwell, Emma Bunton & Melanie Chisholm.

a - bout the fox that I've been chas - ing. He's re - sis - tant not per - sis - tent,

it did - n't stop me from hom - ing in, be - cause I'm choos - y not a flooz - y,

I get my hit and then I run with it. Last time lov - er,

do you think I'm real - ly cool and sex - y, and I know you want to get with me.

last time lov - er treat me right, lov - in' un - der cov - er all night.

Cool sex-y, ev-er rea-dy, some-one fine, al-ways stea-dy, gen-tle hands, dir-ty mind, use your head and don't be

blind, words of love— they don't wash with me, what's the hard rush? No ur - gen-cy you see,

Cra - zy boy, po - ten - tial lov - er, first and last, lov - er broth - er, ain't no oth - er,

crazy, sweet-sy, cool but ra-cy, stea-dy, rea-dy, go, yes!

Last time lov - - - er,

do you think I'm real-ly cool and sex-y? And I know you want to get with me.

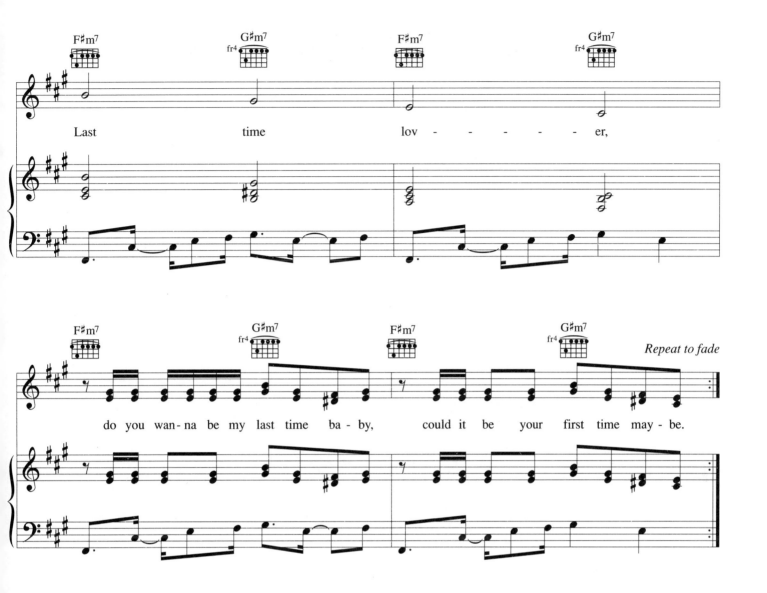

Verse 2:
We got up and down to do it, like the dirty bass in the music,
I got my major chords strummin' took some time and then we're really buzzin',
First bite wet my appetite, second helping's always better,
Started getting burning hot, I found my pride not easy, slowed it down I said stop.
Last time lover…

who do you think you are?

Words & Music by Paul Wilson, Andy Watkins, Melanie Brown,
Victoria Aadams, Geri Halliwell, Emma Bunton & Melanie Chisholm.

1. The race is on to get out of the bot-tom, the top is high so your

(Verse 2 see block lyric)

su-per-star, you____ have got____ to swing it, shake it, move it, make it,

who do you think you are?_____ Trust it, use it, prove it, groove it,

show me how good you are._____ Swing it, shake it, move it, make it,

who do you think you are?_____ Trust it, use it, prove it, groove it,

show how good you are.——

You have got to reach——

—— on up, nev-er lose your soul.————

You have got to reach— on up, nev-er lose con-trol.———— I said

Verse 2:
You're swelling out in the wrong direction,
You've got the bug, superstar you've been bitten,
Your trumpet's blowing for far too long,
Climbing the snake of the ladder, but you're wrong.

I said who do you think you are?
Some kind of superstar,
You have got to swing it, shake it, move it, make it, who do you think you are?
Trust it, use it, prove it, groove it, show me how good you are,
Swing it, shake it, move it, make it, who do you think you are?
Trust it, use it, prove it, groove it, show how good you are.

something kinda funny

Words & Music by Paul Wilson, Andy Watkins, Melanie Brown,
Victoria Aadams, Geri Halliwell, Emma Bunton & Melanie Chisholm.

some - thing kind - a fun - ny go - in' on.

Wher - ev - er you're go - ing, high or low, re - mem - ber to
(Verse 2 see block lyric)

sure en - joy the show, so climb a - board my jour - ney deep in - side,

bet - ter late than dead on time, ooh, it's

Verse 2:
Happiness is just a state of your mind,
Keep searching who knows what you may find,
Rules are for fools, and fool's paradise is hard to find,
Play my game or get left behind,
It's you I know that I have got to feed,
Take from me what you feel that you need,
You feel that you need.

We've got something kinda funny goin' on,
We've got something kinda funny goin' on.

You've got it…
Feelin' kinda funny,
Feelin' kinda queasy,
I ain't that easy.

We've got something kinda funny goin' on.

naked

Words & Music by Paul Wilson, Andy Watkins, Melanie Brown,
Victoria Aadams, Geri Halliwell, Emma Bunton & Melanie Chisholm.

ï-ve-ty and child-hood left be-hind, de-prived of the good-ness of man-kind,
(Verses 2 & 3 see block lyric)

past en-coun-ters have made her strong, strong e-nough to car-ry on and on,

un-dress you with her eyes, un-cov-er the truth from the lies,

strip you down don't need to care, lights are low, ex-posed and bare.

Na-

N.C.

Spoken: Hello, it's me. I thought you'd understand. Well, maybe I should have kept my big mouth shut.
I keep seeing such a pretty picture, but I'd rather be hated than pitied.
Maybe I should have left it to your own imagination. I just want to be me.

⊕ Coda

na - ked,___ noth - ing but a smile___ up - on her

face,___ she wants to play seek_ and hide, no - one to hide_ be - hind,

___ this child has fall - en___ from

Verse 2:

Naked,
She knows exactly what to do with men like you, inside out in her mind there's
No doubt where you're coming from, mystery will turn you on.
Undress you with her eyes, uncover the truth from the lies,
Strip you down, don't need to care, lights are low, exposed and bare.

Naked,
Nothing but a smile upon her face.
Naked,
She wants to play seek and hide, no-one to hide behind.
Naked,
This child has fallen from grace.
Naked,
Don't be afraid to stare, she is only naked.

Verse 3:

This angel's dirty face is sore, holding on to what she had before.
Not sharing secrets with any old fool, now she's gonna keep her cool.
She wants to get naked,
She wants to get naked.

Naked,
Nothing but a smile upon her face.
Naked,
She wants to play seek and hide, no-one to hide behind.
Naked,
This child has fallen from grace.
Naked,
Don't be afraid to stare, she is only naked.

if u can't dance

Words & Music by Matthew Rowbottom, Richard Stannard, Melanie Brown,
Victoria Aadams, Geri Halliwell, Emma Bunton, Melanie Chisholm, Bootsy Collins,
Gregory Jacobs, George Clinton & William Morrison.

if you can't dance to this, you can't do noth-ing for— me ba - by. 1. Now

we got the fla-vour, the bad be-ha-viour, the rhy-thm, the me-lo-dy, the juice for you to sa-vour,
(2º Spanish rap see block lyric)

rock-in' and vib-ing, some-bo-dy is jiv - in', you need to take a tip, sort it out, get a grip. When-

ev-er I go out, wher-ev-er it may be, there is nev-er a Ke-a-nu but a dweeb look-in' at me. But then

ev-en if I did score he's a los-er on the dance-floor, take a deep breath count 1, 2,

3.
Ev-en when his eyes met mine, his slam-ming moves were out of time.

Can't you just feel the groove, why don't you move, it's ea-sy can't you see,

take my hands and dance with me.

Spanish rap:
Hey macho te vi otro día me dia mucha mucha alegría,
escucha la música ay madre mia hey chico tu no tienes nada.
Que susto que juego que polla que quieto oh no me tocas ay que perro feo,
venga venga marcha salida toma esta música me canta de prisa.
Cuidado, cuidado que chico que loco toma mi ritmo me voy contigo.
Hey macho te quiero quiero un hombre necesito si pero no tu nombre.
Hey macho, hey macho, si no baila esto no puede sin nada conmigo.

5/97 (278